AWESOME ATHLETES

SHERYL SWOOPES

D1314069

Chris W. Sehnert
ABDO & Daughters

visit us at
www.abdopub.com

Published by Abdo & Daughters, 4940 Viking Drive, Suite 622, Edina, Minnesota 55435.
Copyright © 1998 by Abdo Consulting Group, Inc., Pentagon Tower, P.O. Box 36036, Minneapolis, Minnesota 55435 USA. International copyrights reserved in all countries. No part of this book may be reproduced in any form without written permission from the publisher.

Printed in the United States.

Cover and Interior Photo credits: Duomo
                                     Allsports
                                     Sports Illustrated

Edited by Kal Gronvall

Library of Congress Cataloging-in-Publication Data

Sehnert, Chris W.
   Sheryl Swoopes / Chris Sehnert.
   p. cm. -- (Awesome athletes)
   Includes index.
   Summary: Describes the life and basketball career of the young woman who won a gold medal at the 1996 Olympics and went on to play in the Women's National Basketball Association.
   ISBN 1-56239-845-8
   1. Swoopes, Sheryl--Juvenile literature. 2. Women basketball players--United States--Biography--Juvenile literature. [1. Swoopes, sheryl. 2. Basketball players. 3. Afro-Americans--Biography. 4. Women--Biography.] I. Title. II. Series.
GV884.S88S45   1998
796.323'092--dc 21
   [B]
                                                      97-25522
                                                      CIP
                                                        AC

Contents

Swoopes!

"*Swish!*" is the sound of a basketball falling through the hoop. "*Swoopes!*" is the noise made by basketball fans when one of today's premier athletes is on the court. Sheryl Swoopes is among the very best at what she does. What Sheryl does best is make a basketball go "*swish!*"

Sheryl Swoopes plays basketball for the Houston Comets of the new Women's National Basketball Association (WNBA). As both a college and **Olympic** athlete, she has won nearly every honor made to her. She was named the National Player of the Year in 1993, after leading Texas Tech University to the women's college basketball championship. In 1996, Sheryl won a gold medal with the United States of America's Olympic team.

When Sheryl graduated from college, there were no **professional** women's basketball leagues in America. Without a chance to play basketball at home in America, she traveled to Europe and joined a league in Italy. Living far away from her family and friends was difficult for Sheryl, so she returned to Texas. Back home, she took a job at a local bank before becoming a member of the United States **Olympic** Team.

The great success of the American women's basketball team at the 1996 Summer Olympics in Atlanta, Georgia, gave rise to the idea for a new league. Before long, plans were under way for not one, but two **professional** women's basketball leagues!

Suddenly, Sheryl had to choose between the new American Basketball League (ABL) and the WNBA. While the ABL was first to begin play, Sheryl decided to wait. The WNBA promised to have a team in her home state of Texas. Sheryl has become **internationally** famous for her talent. Now she is swooping and swishing as a professional basketball player in America!

Texas Tornado

Sheryl Denise Swoopes was born on March 25, 1971, in Brownfield, Texas. Brownfield is a small town on the western side of the Texas "Panhandle," 40 miles southwest of Lubbock, Texas. The area around Sheryl's hometown is called the Great Plains. It is known for its production of oil, wheat, and cattle.

The Great Plains of Texas are also known for their high-velocity wind storms. The most destructive winds come from the violent, twirling twisters called tornadoes. When Sheryl began to develop her own twisting, twirling style on the basketball courts of Brownfield, she had a look that was all too familiar. She was known for destroying all rivals in her path. That is why she is nicknamed the "Texas Tornado!"

Sheryl learned to enjoy the game of basketball at an early age. When she was three years old, she would dress up like a cheerleader to watch her older brothers

James and Earl play. By the time she was seven, Sheryl was beginning to join their backyard **scrimmages**. She was the only daughter in a family of four children, and she learned to be strong whenever her brothers teased her. She also learned to **dribble** the ball so that no one could take it away from her!

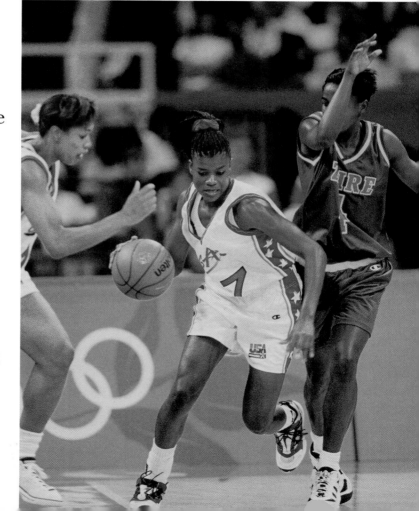

Sheryl Swoopes dribbling the ball for the United States Women's Olympic Basketball Team.

Sheryl's mother was also a strong person. Louise Swoopes raised her children without the help of her husband Billy, who left the family when Sheryl was a small child. Louise worked two jobs to provide what she could for her family. Times were tough, and the kids learned to make the best out of what they had. An old bicycle wheel tacked to a plywood plank became the Swoopes' hoop. Sheryl's mother always told them that their school work had to be finished before the backyard battles under the hoop began.

At the age of nine, Sheryl led her Little Dribblers basketball team to the national championship tournament in Beaumont, Texas. Traveling across the state to watch Sheryl play turned out to be the family's first vacation. Sheryl was growing fast, and her teammates nicknamed her "Legs." Their loss in the tournament's final game was a big disappointment at the time. The Texas Tornado had begun to stir. It wasn't long before Sheryl Swoopes would take the world by storm!

One of the Boys?

When Sheryl was growing up, most people thought basketball was a sport for boys only. There were no **professional** women's basketball leagues in America. Girls were not urged to be athletes. Many schools didn't even have teams for girls. Sheryl, however, loved the game. She often found that the only way to get better was to practice with the boys.

During the summertime, Sheryl would spend three nights a week at the high school gym. She worked hard to earn the respect of the male players, but she was not always welcome to play. When they made fun of her, she would get angry and sometimes thought about giving up. In the end, though, her hard work was rewarded. She made the varsity girl's basketball team at Brownfield High School as a ninth-grader!

In high school, Sheryl turned into an all-around great athlete. She set a school record for the long jump in track and field, and her growing height proved to be helpful on the volleyball court as well as on the basketball court. As a **junior**, Sheryl led the Brownfield Lady Cubs basketball team to the State High School Championship, and she was named the Player-of-the-Year in the state of Texas!

Sheryl graduated from high school in 1989. She had already said yes to a basketball **scholarship** from the University of Texas. When she arrived the next fall on the Longhorns' **campus** in Austin, Texas, she was not ready for her new life. Texas is a big state, and the city of Austin is a long way from the tiny town of Brownfield. Sheryl didn't like being away from her family. She flew home after one week and did not want to go back.

It was hard for Sheryl to leave the University of Texas. She knew she had let down the Lady Longhorns basketball team. She wanted to keep playing the game she loved, so she signed up for classes at a small school just 30 miles outside of Brownfield, called the South Plains Community College.

With the South Plains Lady Texans basketball team, Sheryl was twice named as a **Junior College All-American**. She set 15 school records in those two seasons, and in 1991 was named the Junior College Player-of-the-Year. Sheryl would later say that during those two years, she was most proud of beating her brothers on the family's backyard court. She had finally proven that she was not just one of the boys. She was better!

Sheryl Swoopes played college basketball for South Plains Community College.

Red Raiders

After two years of **junior college**, Sheryl accepted a **scholarship** to join the Texas Tech Lady Red Raiders. Texas Technological University is in the city of Lubbock, Texas. Lubbock was much closer to her home than the capital city of Austin had been. With Sheryl playing for Lubbock's Red Raiders, a showdown against the Lady Longhorns of Austin was bound to happen.

The University of Texas and Texas Tech University are both members of the **NCAA's** Southwest Conference. The Longhorns have been a powerhouse in women's college basketball for many years and won the 1986 National Championship. Texas Tech had never won a conference title before Sheryl Swoopes came along.

During Sheryl's two seasons with Texas Tech, the Lady Red Raiders had a 58-8 record and won the Southwest Conference Title both years! Her final game against the University of Texas Lady Longhorns came in the 1993

Conference Championship. Sheryl scored a career-high 53 points that day. That winning game put the Lady Red Raiders in their second straight appearance in the **NCAA** Tournament.

In 1992, the Red Raiders lost in the NCAA Tournament to the National Champions from Stanford University. The next season, however, Texas Tech was not to be denied. Sheryl won her second Southwest Conference Player-of-the-Year Award, and was named the Most Valuable Player of the NCAA **Final Four**. Sheryl Swoopes was the Most Outstanding Player-of-the-Year in all of women's college basketball.

After four straight wins in the 1993 NCAA Tournament, the Lady Red Raiders met the Ohio State Buckeyes in the championship game. Sheryl made 47 points that night, which broke the 20-year-old record for scoring in an NCAA Championship. Bill Walton was the former record holder and is now a member of the Basketball **Hall of Fame**. Texas Tech's 84-82 victory made Sheryl's Red Raiders the 1993 National Champions.

THE MAKING OF AN AWESOME ATHLETE

Sheryl Swoopes on defense.

1971

Born March 25 in Brownfield, Texas.

1988

Won State Championship for Brownfield High. Named Player of the Year.

1989

Attends South Plains Community College.

1991

Named Junior College Player of the Year.

How Awesome Is She?

Sheryl Swoopes has had an incredible career to this point, with many more years to go in the WNBA. Here are some reasons why Swoopes is such an awesome athlete.

- Led Texas Tech to 58-8 record in two seasons.
- Averaged 13 points, 3.5 rebounds, and 3.9 assists while playing in the 1996 Atlanta Games.
- Set an NCAA record with 47 points in one game against Ohio State in 1993.

SHERYL SWOOPES

TEAM: HOUSTON COMETS
NUMBER: 1
POSITION: GUARD/FORWARD
HEIGHT: 6 FEET
WEIGHT: 145 POUNDS

1993	1993	1996	1997
Wins second Southwest Conference player of the Year.	Named NCAA Final Four MVP.	Won a Gold Medal for USA in the 1996 Olympics.	Signs with the Houston Comets in the new WNBA League.

- **1988 High School Player of the Year for the state of Texas.**
- **1991 Named Junior College Player of the Year.**
- **1993 Named Southwest Conference Player of the Year.**
- **Voted MVP of the 1993 NCAA Final Four.**
- **Won the Gold Medal for Basketball in the 1996 Olympics.**

Highlights

Air Sheryl

Sheryl's final season of college basketball named her as the top female in the sport. People thought her high-flying style was a lot like Michael "Air" Jordan's style. The great champion of the Chicago Bulls is among the finest to have ever played the game. Michael is also one of the game's greatest **ambassadors**. In 1993, Sheryl Swoopes was named by the Women's Sports Foundation as their Sportswoman-of-the-Year.

If there had been a **professional** woman's basketball league in America in 1993, Sheryl would have been one of the first players selected. But there wasn't, yet. Sheryl decided to take her talents overseas. She joined a professional team in the Italian Women's Basketball League, but after just 10 games she again was lonely for her family and friends. Sheryl averaged 23 points per game during her short stay in Europe. In October, she left Bari, Italy, and went back to Brownfield, Texas.

Back home, Sheryl took a job at a local bank. She began delivering **radio commentary** on women's athletics and also played in several off-season basketball camps. She soon played as a member of a few United States **amateur** teams for their **international** tournaments. She won a bronze medal with the USA Team during the 1994 World Championships at Sydney, Australia, and a gold medal at the Goodwill Games in St. Petersburg, Florida.

Among the many basketball camps Sheryl went to during those years, one was held by Michael Jordan. Sheryl and Michael shared similar styles on the basketball court. They were both playmakers and top scorers for their teams. When Michael asked to play against her one-on-one, Sheryl could not pass up the game.

The game was played before a television audience and a full-house of excited people. Sheryl scored the first three points before Michael kicked himself into high gear and beat her 7-5. "His Airness" ended the contest with a high-flying slam dunk and shook hands with Sheryl for her hard work on the court.

Sheryl Swoopes had become the most well known woman in basketball. The attention people gave to Sheryl started to pave the way for a **professional** women's basketball league in America. She had become a **spokesperson** for women's athletics, and her picture began to appear on major product **endorsements**, like *Kellogg's Corn Flakes.*

In 1995, Sheryl became the first female athlete to have a shoe named after her. The *Nike* company has enjoyed a long success with their basketball shoes named after Michael Jordan. When they designed a line for women, they called their new shoes *"Air Swoopes!"*

Opposite page: Swoopes in action for the Olympic team.

Golden Girls

Sheryl has always loved watching the **Olympics**. As a girl growing up in Texas, the female athletes who were in the **international** festival of games were her favorite **role models**. Bringing home a gold medal for the United States of America was one of her childhood dreams.

In the spring of 1992, Sheryl worked hard to earn a spot on the American women's basketball team for their Olympic competition in Barcelona, Spain. She was cut from the roster when an ankle injury stopped her from finishing the tryouts. Four years later, Sheryl Swoopes joined a group of the finest American women athletes ever brought together on one team.

The 1996 Summer Olympic Games were held in Atlanta, Georgia. The American women's basketball team began practicing more than a year before the festival started. Among the 12 members who made the final cut were the towering pair Lisa Leslie and Rebecca Lobo, long-time leaders Katrina McClain and Teresa Edwards, and a superb ball handler named Jennifer Azzi. With Sheryl's outside shooting and defensive abilities added to the mix, Team USA was unstoppable!

To practice for the big event, the team played a 52 game schedule against the finest teams of college and **international** women's basketball. Team USA won every game! Along the way, they traveled across the United States and played on four continents. The long hours spent on the road and in practice caused the players to grow together as a team. They had become true **ambassadors** for the sport of women's basketball.

On July 19, 1996, the opening ceremonies in Atlanta marked the 100th anniversary of the modern **Olympic** Games. America's finest women basketball players wanted to celebrate the occasion with gold. With seven straight wins they made it to the final match. Their opponents from Brazil were also undefeated and had taken the gold medal at the World Championships two years earlier.

The American crowd greeted Sheryl with calls of "Swoooooopes" each time she touched the ball. They also teased the Brazilian team with chants of "U-S-A!" Every member of the American team scored in the game. The final score was Team USA-111, Brazil-87. The gold medal belonged to America. Sheryl's **Olympic** dream had come true!

Sheryl Swoopes (fourth from left) with the rest of her Olympic teammates.

Choices

The choices a person makes at any time can have a great effect on their life. Chances come and go, and a bad decision may take years to overcome. Female athletes in America have not always been given many chances for playing sports. For many years, the greatest stars of women's college basketball were forced to choose between continuing their careers overseas or giving up the game they loved. The success of the American women's basketball team at the 1996 **Olympics** began to change all of that.

When Sheryl Swoopes chose to leave the University of Texas, many people thought she had given up her chance to win a National Championship. She proved them wrong. When she left Italy, they said she had ruined her chance to play **professional** basketball. Instead, Sheryl returned home to play a big part in the drive to bring professional women's basketball to America.

By the time Team USA's 14 month world tour had come to its glorious end, there were two **professional** women's basketball leagues forming in America. This sudden jump in popularity gave the female **Olympic** champions the choice to keep playing basketball. Some chose to bring their talents to the American Basketball League (ABL), which began play in the fall of 1996. Still others returned to Europe, where the growing demand for their talent made them more valuable than ever before. Sheryl Swoopes was among the members of Team USA who decided to play in the WNBA.

Like so many times before, Sheryl's decision was based on her desire to have a home in Texas. The WNBA was set to begin play in the summer of 1997, and would have a team in Houston. Along with her Olympic teammates Lisa Leslie and Rebecca Lobo, Sheryl was among the first players chosen for the new league. Each of the players would begin their professional careers near the towns where they started playing. Sheryl Swoopes became a member of the Houston Comets.

Sheryl had more choices to make outside of basketball. In June, 1995, she married her high school sweetheart Eric Jackson. When the **Olympics** were over, Sheryl and Eric found out they would be parents. In June of 1997, they had a boy and named him Jordan—after another great basketball player. Because of the new baby Sheryl started later in the season with the Comets. The Comets were glad to have her on board. By Sheryl's third game back she was averaging double figures in scoring and assists!

Sheryl Swoopes leading the fast break.

25

Bringing It All Back Home

Sheryl Swoopes is among the very best at what she does. She has been compared to a Texas Tornado for her lightning fast moves on the basketball court. Her long jump shots are fired with deadly accuracy, and her quickness on defense is equally destructive to her rivals. Sheryl has come a long way from the backyard **scrimmages** with her brothers to the wake of her new career as a **professional** basketball player in America.

Times were tough when Sheryl was growing up. Louise Swoopes struggled every day to provide food and shelter for her children. Sheryl struggled for acceptance, as a girl trying to succeed at a "boys game." She has never forgotten those hard times, or the times when she wondered if giving up her dream was the best choice.

Sheryl Swoopes prepares to shoot a free throw.

Through all of her successes she has never lost her sense of home and family.

Basketball's popularity as a women's sporting event has never been greater. That popularity has come through the sacrifice and dedication of players like Sheryl Swoopes. Their journey has only begun. The success of women's **professional** basketball in America will depend on the support of the people who appreciate great talent.

There are two sounds these fans hear whenever the Houston Comets are in town. The first, the sound of "*Swooopes*," is the noise made when the player with the popularity of Michael Jordan has the ball. The second is the sound of "*swish*," when Sheryl nets another on her way to basketball history.

Glossary

All-American - A person chosen as the best amateur athlete at her position.

Amateur - A person who performs without being paid.

Ambassador - A person whose mission is to help others appreciate what they represent.

Campus - The grounds surrounding an institution such as a school or hospital.

Dribble - To advance the ball in basketball through repeated bouncing.

Endorsement - To sell one's name or image in support of a product.

Final Four - The four teams who reach the semi-final round of a tournament.

Hall of Fame - A memorial for the greatest players of all time.

International - Belonging to more than one nation or to all nations of the world.

Junior - A student in the third year of a U.S. high school or college.

Junior College - An institution of higher learning that offers two year certificate programs.

NCAA (National Collegiate Athletic Association) - An organization that oversees the administration of college athletics.

Olympics - An international festival of athletic contests held every four years in a different city.

Professional - A person who is paid for her work.

Radio Commentary - To submit comments or opinions for radio broadcast.

Role Model - A person who through her characteristics or abilities is in a position to be imitated by others.

Scholarship - A grant given to a student to pay for her college tuition.

Scrimmage - A practice session or informal game.

Spokesperson - A person who speaks on the behalf of her cause.

PASS IT ON

Tell Others Something Special About Your Favorite Sports or Athletes

What makes your favorite athlete awesome? Do you think you have a chance to be an Awesome Athlete? Tell us about your favorite plays, tournaments, and anything else that has to do with sports. We want to hear from you!

To get posted on ABDO & Daughters website E-mail us at "sports@abdopub.com"

Index